# Metaverse & Money

Oscar Smith

Published by J.N.L, 2022.

METAVERSE & MONEY

**First edition. February 27, 2022.**

Copyright © 2022 Oscar Smith.

ISBN: 979-8201096007

Written by Oscar Smith.

# Book Description

The regular 9-5 work cycle is ending and a new revolution is currently dawning on the entire world moment by moment. Many have seen the light of the new day, but yet only a few know how to navigate this new reality to their fortune. The metaverse is a hot topic nowadays, and it is just as tricky as it is hot. Looking up the metaverse and its components on the web gives an idea of what it is and how it works. However, it does not give a contextual analysis. This is to say that it does not place an investor into the entire context of the metaverse. To conceptualize this new reality and fit yourself into it would require extensive research. And with the ever-evolving nature of the metaverse, it is hard to keep up. And if that is not enough of a hurdle in itself, the news keeps piling on top of the building blocks, making the search deeper.

As such, this guide was gathered with the intention of sharing the fundamentals of the metaverse and investing in it. This means that this guide will provide any prospective metaverse investor with solid information on this new and exciting form of investment. By indulging in this guide, prospective metaverse investors will save themselves from endless research—they will not have to tediously sift through endless piles of information in order to find the cornerstones of it all. This is because the creation of this guide entailed carrying out extensive research from reliable sources. As such, the success of any prospective metaverse investor that utilizes this guide will heavily depend on their understanding and commitment to their financial well-being.

# Metaverse & Money

## *A Beginner's Guide into the Digital Future*

# Oscar Smith

# Introduction

The word metaverse is being thrown around a lot lately. Need a conversation starter? Talk about the metaverse. Popular as it is, the metaverse is still as mysterious as the ocean. Plagued with tech language and complex otherworldly concepts, this is a subject that is not easy for any beginner to navigate. What makes it trickier is the plethora of opinions on the entire subject by avowed experts. As if that is not enough, individuals have taken to social media to try and stop the rest of us from selling our souls to this dark revolution. It is like 5G all over again. However, if you are reading this guide, it clearly stands to show that you reject all projected fears and confusion in favor of your financial well-being.

Every revolution the world has witnessed brought with it new ways with which to conceptualize and interact with the world. When Frederick Taylor's specialization theory hit the streets, individuals were tasked with deciding what job they wanted and equipping themselves with the necessary knowledge and skills so as to see to it that they are able to complete their jobs efficiently. When the world shifted from skilled work to industrial work, individuals were tasked with equipping themselves with relevant skills and knowledge in order to equip themselves for whichever occupation they were interested in. The world later shifted to corporate and, even then, individuals were tasked with equipping themselves with the necessary skills and knowledge in order to secure a safe climb up the corporate ladder. This is right around the time where university and college qualifications became of dire importance to the masses.

As of recently, the world is going digital. The pace at which technology has advanced over the past 10 years is exponential. This is moreso the case given that just 10 years ago masses, worldwide, had anticipated the end of the world. Yet, 10 years later the world as we know it is coming to an end. This is yet another revolution, digital in nature, giving a bigger chance at life for everyone than was the case in any of the previous revolutions that the world has witnessed.

Herein lies a virtual world which provides a new start for people of all kinds. In this world, nobody is not forced to fit into a certain box in order to make a success of themselves. Artists do not have to maintain a day job in order to pay bills. Investors do not have to reach deep into their wallets in order to secure a juicy investment. This widens the investment pool for more wallets. Thick, thin, old, and new wallets have a chance at making a profit out of this world and this guide will point into the right direction in this regard.

As a potential investor, there are various ways for you to approach metaverse investing. If you are a gamer, then gaming is the way to go. Similarly, if you are a creator of any sort at all, there are investment opportunities for you too. To add to that, if you are one to fancy making real-world like investments by entering the metaverse and exploring it, then you are catered for.

Before getting into the thick of it, let us lay out the contextual background to metaverse investment. More specifically, what the metaverse is and what powers it. The metaverse is a vast virtual reality, likened to the universe. Within the metaverse, there are countless virtual activities of differing natures and kinds that offer profits that can be valued in the real world; there are also countless other virtual worlds that are referred to as metaverses. These metaverses are usually created for a specific purpose. For instance, a gaming metaverse is a virtual world where users play to earn. There are countless entry points to any metaverse. For instance, you can enter the gaming metaverse through playing one game today or another the next.

What makes metaverse investing stand out is the mere fact that it is all decentralized. This means that everything found in here is for mass benefit. With inherent developments such as Web 3.0, for instance, it is an opportunity for people to own the Internet. Web 3.0 is the third version of the Internet (following Web 1.0 and Web 2.0) where information is both democratized and decentralized. Individuals who have tried monetizing a blog or a vlog personally know the challenges that big companies that own Internet platforms place in front of them. Because of the competition, it is not easy for people who intend to use our current Internet (Web 2.0) to try and make a living. However, since this journey leads into a virtual world that is characterized by decentralization, it removes many odds that are usually found in our real world.

This entire movement into a decentralized, virtual world is powered by blockchain technology. In simple terms, blockchain technology is a public ledger that is distributed in a digital format on a particular network. If a certain game, application, or platform claims to be based on the Ethereum blockchain, then the transactions carried out on it are entered into that public ledger. It is open to the public since anyone who has a computer that is connected to the particular blockchain for review purposes can see all of the transactions.

Much like the Bitcoin train, you stand to lose if you do not jump into this investment opportunity.

# Chapter 1: Blockchain Technology

This virtual revolution has a fully functional economy, all of which is based on blockchain technology. This means that anyone who wishes to interact with the metaverse in any way will have to acquaint themselves with differing products and services by platforms and applications that are placed on the differing blockchains. As of present there exists a handful of blockchains that are prominent. These include the: Bitcoin Blockchain, Ethereum Blockchain, Binance Smart Chain, and Solana Blockchain.

The first thing any potential metaverse investor has to do is to create a virtual wallet. This wallet will be the means through which you receive or make transactions. To add to that, this wallet is key to connecting with a variety of platforms such as marketplaces and applications. For convenience purposes, the wallets to be discussed in this guide are software wallets only. These kinds of wallets are popularly referred to as hot wallets in the cryptocurrency world. These hot wallets come in the form of software and applications to be run on both computers and mobile phones. As such, you have the option to decide on the medium you will use to store and trade your cryptocurrencies.

# Best Cryptocurrency Wallets

There exists a plethora of options when it comes to the topic of wallets. However, there are only a handful of tried and tested wallets that are trusted by many users and platforms. These include:

# MetaMask

Popularly known for being the standard wallet to connect to any online and virtual marketplace, MetaMask works both as a web extension and an application. This cryptocurrency wallet is backed by the Ethereum blockchain. Thus, it allows users to interact with Ethereum-backed platforms and cryptocurrencies. While MetaMask works both as a wallet (to store your cryptocurrencies) and an exchange (to trade your cryptocurrencies), its best feature is its incorporation of Web 3.0. Within the mobile application, you will be able to access the third wave of the Internet. While Web 3.0 covers a vast field, with MetaMask you can count on accessing blockchain-based sites. This will help you cut through all of the popular information on the Internet (by views) to the real information. To add to that, there are no products and services from Web 2.0 monopolists (just you and the information you are looking for).

# Coinbase

Supporting more than 4,000 tokens as well as a plethora of Dapps (decentralized applications), Coinbase is one of the leaders in cryptocurrency wallets. It is also based on the Ethereum Blockchain and boasts industry-leading security measures. This is because the Coinbase wallet puts the security measures in the control of its users. Often referred to as self-custodial, this wallet lets you store your private keys on your device. Your private keys are a representation of the cryptocurrencies that you are holding in your wallet. This wallet is made for individuals who want to have a full sense of control over their affairs. While the local storage of a user's private keys has received major criticism from people worldwide, Coinbase continues to give determined users a safe haven. With this wallet, the safety depends entirely on you in the same way that your funds do.

# Binance (Trust Wallet)

This is a cryptocurrency wallet initiated by one of the world's prominent cryptocurrency exchanges—Binance. It is based on both the Binance Smart Chain and Ethereum, which shows that it is more versatile in nature of transacting. It takes the form of a web extension and serves the primary purposes of sending and receiving funds on both Binance's and Ethereum's blockchains. However, if you are looking to do more with a wallet within the Binance Blockchain, then the Trust Wallet is the way to go. Having been acquired by Binance, Trust Wallet is now the official cryptocurrency wallet for Binance.

Trust wallet was recently acquired by Binance in 2018, and is now its official exchange mobile wallet. Binance enhanced this top Ethereum wallet to even bigger heights with features such as Trust Wallet's support for 14 different blockchains, and has also added the feature of cold storage to this wallet. Binance is stretching this wallet so far and wide it might eliminate the need for any other wallet in the near future (since this one will be able to perform most, if not all, wallet features).

# Crypto.com

Much like the Coinbase wallet, Crypto.com offers a wallet that is in full custody of its user. Not only do you control your funds, but you also get a handle on your private keys. The Crypto.com App, however, is a custodian of your cryptocurrencies. As such, be sure to go for the wallet and not the app if you're looking to have a full sense of control over your investments. This is the right wallet for people who actually want to go into trading their cryptocurrencies. If you are looking to do more than just buy, hold, and sell then this wallet gives you such freedoms. It offers highly competitive fees and its routine discounts make it a sore sight for its competitors. However, in order to leverage these competitive prices, you have to use the platform's native coin—CRO.

Now that the wallets are out of the way, it is essential for you to know your marketplaces. Marketplaces based on the blockchain make it easier to purchase and sell your blockchain-based assets—these assets are referred to as non-fungible tokens (NFTs) since an owner has to mint them before entering them in the marketplaces. Therefore, the marketplaces on which these digital assets are traded are referred to as NFT marketplaces.

# Best NFT Marketplaces

# Opensea

This marketplace has taken the lead in the sales of non-fungible tokens worldwide for years. With a vast variety of digital assets on their platform, their signup process is free to anyone who wants to partake in trades on this prominent market. It also has a minting process for creators of all sorts. As if that is not enough, this marketplace supports over 150 tokens used for payment purposes.

# CryptoPunks

Gaining its popularity in the community due to its NFT project that sold for millions, Crypto Punks is now a widely respected non-fungible token marketplace. This marketplace focused on releasing digital art projects, with its most recent being Autoglyphs. While the original Crypto Punk NFTs have sold out, they can be bid on and acquired from a variety of other third party marketplaces. Other projects such as the Meebits are also lucrative assets listed on the marketplace. Lastly, be on the lookout for any other application development projects that are based on the Ethereum blockchain.

# Axie Marketplace

If you indulge yourself in the Axie Infinity virtual reality, you will have this marketplace at your disposal. On this marketplace, you can buy the metaverse's local beasts, called *Axies*—all of which differ in power and skills. These local beasts are collected by players during quests and such, and then they are pitted against one another in battles between players who own them. This marketplace also sells Axie Infinity land as well as any other NFT that is associated with this virtual game.

# Rarible

Similar to Opensea, this marketplace hase a vast variety of digital assets. On top of being able to list many digital assets, this platform also provides minting services for artists and asset owners. The point of departure from Opensea is that you need to use the token indeginous to the marketplace, called *Rarible*. This token is used as a medium of exchange on the marketplace.

# NBA Top Shot Marketplace

The National Basketball Association, together with the Women's National Basketball Association, transitioned the world of sports into new forms of monetization such as listing their plays on the marketplace. This marketplace sells collectible moments taken from iconic plays by NBA players. These video clips and highlights from premiere basketball leagues can be traded as art.

# Nifty Giveaway

World renowned assets such as Beeple have had their sales facilitated by the Nifty Giveaway Marketplace. This stands to show its reliability. Created to be an art curation platform, Nifty Giveaway is powered by Gemini (the cryptocurrency exchange). The digital assets minted and sold on this platform are known as *Nifties*, and they are built on the Ethereum blockchain. When you purchase a Niftie here, it is stored for you by both the platform as well as Gemini. If you do not have any Ethereum in your wallet, you can purchase some using your fiat currency.

# Foundation

Originally created as a platform to make hassle-free bids, Foundation has now evolved into one of the best non-fungible token marketplaces. Within less than a year after launching, this marketplace has generated over $10 million sales on minted digital assets.

# Superare

Much like Rarible, this platform is targeting digital creators. As such, this marketplace is a hub for all forms of artists. However, what would a marketplace without buyers be? As such, buyers who have Ethereum in their wallets are free to come indulge in and take possession of the finest art in the virtual lands.

# ThetaDrop

This marketplace stems from a blockchain-based platform that is only concerned with the decentralized distribution of video and television on the Internet. Theta Drop debuted in 2021 through the digital collectibles from the World Poker Tour. Since this marketplace is based on its own marketplace, it is essential to purchase its local cryptocurrency, called *Theta Token*. Theta Drop is backed by bigger platforms, such as Binance, and the cryptocurrencies secured herein can be stored in a digital wallet (it has its own wallet as well).

# Mintable

Supported by billionaire Mark Cuban, this marketplace aims at surpassing the leading marketplace, called Opensea. Using Ethereum as its main cryptocurrency for trading, Mintable's platform supports a vast variety of digital asset owners. It even has space for musicians and other forms of artists to mint their artwork and sell it on the marketplace.

If you have your eyes set on minting your art and are not sure how you can transfer your physical art into digital art, then there exist two options for you. Firstly, take pictures of your assets and then upload them into your personal computer; then secondly, upload to any of these marketplaces from there. This works for paintings of all sorts, and also photography. If you are a musician, then all you have to do is make sure that your music is of good quality and then list it up there.

# Chapter 2: Contextual Background

Since earnings from these investments are measured in cryptocurrency (instead of fiat currency), it is key to grasp the concept of cryptocurrency holistically. Cryptocurrency is virtual currency. This is a currency that seldom has any physical representation and usually takes the form of coins and tokens in the virtual world. While cryptocurrency was originally known to have no physical representations at all, newer developments have pioneered objects such as cryptocurrency credit cards in the real world. These coins and tokens exist on a public and decentralized ledger known as the blockchain. It should be clear by now that there are a variety of blockchains in existence (Bitcoin, Ethereum, Binance, etc.). Therefore, cryptocurrencies exist on public and decentralized ledgers where any transaction made using them is recorded on the blockchain they are based on. This digital payment system does not rely on central authorities, such as banks, in order to verify payments. Instead, it relies on a peer-to-peer network where anyone with a crypto wallet and mining hardware (as well as mining software) can verify (mine) transactions made on the blockchain.

Simply put, to mine is to verify transactions by way of checking if the sender has enough cryptocurrency to complete the transaction and whether the receiver is on the said blockchain. Verified transactions are then added to the decentralized ledger they took place on. To add to that, the main benefit of this system is to avoid duplicate transactions where the sender mistakenly makes the same payment twice. With Bitcoin, potential miners have to be verified in that regard so as to see to it that digital platforms are not manipulated in any way—which creates responsible miners. The incentive that lies herein is receipt of newly minted coins; this is what attracts miners to this profession. And it's a competitive profession, since it works on a first-come, first-serve basis. A prospective miner has to possess equipment that is able to address and process cryptographic data at speeds that will almost always guarantee them first place in cracking the codes behind cryptocurrency transactions. These pieces of equipment are not necessarily easy on the wallet, though.

# Metaverses

It is essential to acquaint yourself with the types of metaverses within this virtual universe. Or simply put, know the virtual worlds that can be found inside this virtual universe. The most dominant and well-known kinds of metaverses include:

# Gaming Metaverses

These metaverses are growing exponentially and gaining a lot of traction. This is because new and fully immersive virtual reality games are transitioning into the metaverse, giving players the opportunity to monetize their virtual adventures. Because of this, gone are the days when your gaming avatar was rich while you were struggling to make ends meet in real life. These virtual worlds provide a vast variety of gaming adventures for both heavyweight and lightweight gamers. If you are a heavyweight gamer, then there are extremely immersive adventures in games such as Illuvium. On the other hand, if you are a lightweight gamer, then there are games such as Axies Infinity that are not too hectic but just as engaging.

# Art Metaverse

Regardless of the kind of art they produce, artists stand to make worthy earnings within the metaverse. From music to all forms of visual arts to newly found virtual art, every artist can monetize their art. Art metaverses are not usually found as a metaverse on their own (like gaming). Instead, they usually coexist with another virtual world. In metaverses that specialize with land and its developments (such as Decentraland), a user may bump into a variety of art exhibitions and museums. This is where artists make it a point to have their pieces of art listed. In the virtual world, there are also more direct points of interactions where artists place their pieces. For instance, a musician can mint their song as a non-fungible token and have it listed on Opensea (a prominent virtual NFT marketplace).

Art is a crucial part of any society, and the virtual society is no different. However, the star feature of art in the metaverse is that it can be traded for a worth that its creator feels is fair. A prominent digital artist, Beeple, shocked the world when he sold his art for $69 million. This art was a minted NFT of a collage of 5,00o images that were created throughout a time span of 13 years. This stands to show that the value, effort, and consistency that an artist puts into their work can reap them a rewarding value.

# Fashion Metaverse

Much like the art metaverse, the fashion metaverse exists in conjunction with a complementary metaverse. On marketplaces such as Opensea, it is easy to spot fashion lines and items from completely virtual fashion brands such as FabeeoBreen. On the contrary, there are also fashion brands that have gone virtual for the main purpose of providing potential shoppers with the opportunity to virtually fit their clothes before adding them to the cart. However, those that are concerned with the metaverse exist mainly for the benefit of all the avatars that are found within a particular virtual world. The fashion metaverse enables users to style their avatars and wearable developers in order to make a profit. RTFKT (pronounced artifact) was owned by a youngster who created virtual sneakers for avatars that became so sensational that the company was acquired by Nike. RTFKT sold $3.1 million worth of virtual sneakers in just 7 minutes, which stands to show the immense wealth that stems from the fashion industry within the metaverse. However, this should come as no major surprise due to the fact that the fashion industry in the real world is currently worth $2.5 trillion. Therefore, the success of RTFKT follows suit.

# Industrial Metaverse

There are metaverses that are more serious in nature when compared to their popular counterparts. An industrial metaverse is a virtual world within which bog industry business is carried out. For instance, motor vehicle production companies—such as Audi—create a blueprint version of their soon-to-be-physical creation within a virtual world. There will be simulations and conditions that are similar to the real world that will serve the purposes of quality assurance and so forth. Having a digital blueprint or twin of a physical creation before manufacturing eliminates error and provides maintenance systems of a higher caliber.

On a lighter note, there have been developments in this metaverse that are a mix between our reality and virtual reality in the most literal sense ever. These are developments such as Microsoft's Hololens, which helps professionals and artisans in the manufacturing setting to work through production with the help of their device.

Meta, formerly known as Facebook, has also taken to this metaverse through initiating 3d meeting platforms powered by blockchain technology. Similar initiatives that already exist are Zoom virtual meetings as well as Google Meets. However, Meta aims to go even further by creating an entire digital workplace where employees log in as their own avatars and share interactions and normal work activities within this virtual workplace. As can be seen, this is a step further than our current workplace technology.

# Social Metaverse

Meta has, once more, sought to take social interactions into the metaverse. Despite the fact that the developments are all in the pipeline, it is a lucrative investment for any growth-oriented investor. If you are wondering how you will gain from investing in a social metaverse, then look to life as we know it.

Before diving into the metaverse, you have to find how you fit into the picture. This means that you have to actively seek out what kind of investor you will be. Will you be hands-on? Are you interested in just long-term investments? Do you want in on the action? Furthermore, in determining the kind of investments you intend on carrying out within the metaverse, you have to also know the different ways of investing in the metaverse. There are direct and indirect investing methods.

# Direct Methods of Investing in the Metaverse

# Metaverse Tokens

Metaverses usually have their own local cryptocurrencies, which usually take the form of a token. Sandbox, one of the most prominent real estate metaverses, uses the *SAND* token as its local cryptocurrency. Axie Infinity uses the *AXS* token as its virtual world's local cryptocurrency. These tokens serve foundational purposes in their respective metaverses. The AXS token, for instance, can be utilized by players to decide on the future of the game; and the SAND token serves utility purposes such as completing transactions. In whichever metaverse you join, you can participate in activities, games and build experiences that will help you to earn the respective metaverse's local cryptocurrency. You can use this local cryptocurrency to make purchases in-game, buy advancements, build real estate (if you are in a real estate metaverse), and carry out transactions unique to that metaverse. These tokens can be exchanged into mainstream cryptocurrency coins like Bitcoin and Ethereum and used for the same purposes. As can be seen, this is an option for individuals who would like to interact with the metaverse.

# Non-fungible Tokens

A non-fungible token, popularly referred to as an NFT, is a unit of data that is stored on a blockchain. The data herein often entails digital assets such as virtual land, virtual apparel, music, art, photographs, and videos (to name the most obvious). An NFT can also hold data of objects from our real world such as physical forms of visual art (paintings). This unit of data is stored on the blockchain the moment it is created, sold, or bought. It is essential to note that it comes at a cost—although not too hectic. When minting your work into an NFT, you have to pay fees in order to list it in the marketplace. These fees will depend on factors such as the kind of cryptocurrency you want to use. If you are selling an item using Ethereum as its cryptocurrency, you have to pay the associated fees to get your item stored on the Ethereum blockchain. These fees are usually administered by the marketplace you are using, whether in-game (like the Decentraland marketplace) or independent (like Opensea).

What makes an NFT stand out is the fact that the holder of a particular NFT, be it the buyer or seller, is the only one with ownership rights to the digital asset it represents. This means that no two people can buy the same thing, an error often found in our real world. These ownership rights are far from those in our real world where a person can fabricate a document proving ownership (or even bribe authenticators to prove ownership). This is because NFTs are based on the blockchain, which means that all of the transactions regarding the digital assets completed on the blockchain cannot be tampered with in any way. As a result, non-fungible tokens are solid tokens.

# Virtual Land

Virtual land has been a major attraction to the metaverse. This is because many see it as another chance at developing, conquering, and marking the world. The only difference is that it is all in a virtual universe where some worlds are adventure-based while others are cut-up virtual slices of our real world. The main thing with virtual land is to create experiences and make a living off them.

There are many lucrative uses for virtual land. For starters, you can rent out your piece of land to someone else and earn via that rent. Or, you can build on that specific piece of land and utilize your developments to create lucrative experiences. Snoop Dog, for instance, has acquired land within the Sandbox metaverse and is inviting people over to his virtual party by way of purchasing tokens to share in that particular experience.

You can purchase land as an NFT on any NFT marketplace, buy it from a selling user, or even buy it when the said metaverse releases its land up for auction.

If you are not looking to roll up your sleeves and fully immerse yourself into this investment, then there are investment opportunities for you. These are referred to as indirect investment opportunities.

# Indirect Methods of Investing in the Metaverse

37

# Metaverse Stocks

With a decentralized virtual paradise in the horizons, many companies are charging to have their slice of the never-ending pie. With the removed cap on creativity, many companies are looking to give users an experience like no other. The right mindset to have when approaching stocks would be the one expressed through the phrase, "out with the old, in with the new." However, to avoid risks from investing in a completely new company on a new endeavor, it would be simpler to invest in new paths explored by already trusted companies. Commonly referred to as blue chip companies, these are companies that have proven a successful record. The fact that they are embarking on a new journey means heightened levels of financial gains for anyone who has invested. These include:

# Meta

Formerly known as Facebook, this company has motioned the attention of its millions of users toward the metaverse. What makes Meta rank at top position is the fact that it has announced many amazing projects that are currently in the pipeline.

# Unity

This company is a world leader in the field of 3D software, and it is so formidable that it is claimed that its software is responsible for a majority of the 3D environments in the metaverse.

# Nvidia

Popularly known for its Graphics Processing Units, this company's Omniverse Enterprise has attracted hundreds of companies to it within a short amount of time. As a result, this 3D software company stands as a lucrative investment opportunity for those that are interested in powering the metaverse environment.

# Cloudflare

This company claims that its network delivers content at speeds as high as 50 milliseconds. To add to that, it succeeds in providing cybersecurity services—blocking over 50 billion threats on a daily basis.

# Roblox

This company has already created a virtual world in which artists such as Lil Nas X and Tai Verdes have hosted virtual concerts. With close to 50 million daily users, this metaverse is yet to expand, making it an attractive investment opportunity.

# Index Funds

The second and prominent method of indirectly investing in the metaverse is through an index fund. An index fund is a bundle of stocks from companies that constitute that said index. With an index fund, an investor is automatically diversifying their investment. The purpose of this fund is to mirror the market in which those said companies are focused. As of present, the current index fund on the metaverse is the Metaverse Index, which was created by Index Coop. This index fund comprises of the following companies:

- ENJ: 15.3%

- MANA: 11.8%

- SAND: 9.4%

- AUDIO: 7.5%

- WAXE: 7.4%

- RFOX: 6.5%

- NFTX: 5.8%

- AXS: 5.6%

- DG: 5.6%

- WHALE: 4.8%

- TVK: 4.6%

- REVV: 4.0%

- MEME: 4.0%

- RARI: 3.9%

- MUSE: 3.8%

The major benefits of investing in this index fund include:

- it is simple

- it manages risk

- it is cost effective

- it is transparent

# Chapter 3: Getting Started

As highlighted earlier on, it is clear that there are a few steps and processes to be carried out first before jumping right into making the investments. These include steps on setting up your accounts and wallets. The first steps to be discussed in this chapter are those associated with setting up your MetaMask accounts—this chapter focuses mainly on this cryptocurrency wallet because it is widely used in platforms and endeavors associated with the metaverse.

# Setting Up Your MetaMask Wallet Extension

1. Download the MetaMask wallet extension to your Chrome browser.
2. Install MetaMask for Chrome.
3. After landing on the MetaMask homepage (redirected), click on "Add to Chrome."
4. Open the MetaMask extension by navigating to it on the extension bar on your browser's navigation bar, which will redirect you to MetaMask's welcome page.
5. Click on the "Get Started" button on the welcome page in order to get redirected to the "New to MetaMask" page.
6. On the "New to MetaMask" page, users with existing MetaMask accounts will have the option to import their wallets. Users who are completely new to the platform will have the option to create their wallet.
7. Read and agree to the terms and conditions on the "Help us improve MetaMask" page as the final step to creating your account.
8. Create the password to your MetaMAsk wallet and then read and agree to the terms of use.
9. Watch the video on securing your MetaMask wallet through recovery phrases and then press next to land on the "Secret Recovery—Phrase" page.
10. Click to reveal the secret words included in your recovery phrase; store the phrase in a secure place and press next.
11. Confirm your secret recovery phrase.
12. All done! Start using MetaMask.

Please make it a point that you have a personal copy of your secret recovery phrase stored away safely. Without this phrase, you cannot access your account should it happen that you have installed the application or web extension on another device. The steps discussed above are similar to those to be followed when dealing with a MetaMask mobile application.

The second best option is Coinbase, mainly because it has both a hosted wallet and a self custody wallet. A hosted wallet is a digital wallet that stores a user's private keys with a trusted third party. A self-custodial wallet is a digital wallet where users store their own private keys offline.

# Steps to Setting Up Your Coinbase Wallet (Self-Custodial Wallet)

1. Download the wallet from its website.
2. Install the wallet and press "Create New Wallet."
3. Enter your username. Think it through since you can never change it again.
4. Securely back up your 12 word recovery phrase.
5. Verify and ensure that your recovery phrase has been saved.
6. Create a password to use for accessing your wallet.
7. All done! Use your Coinbase Wallet.

Since this is a custodial wallet, please prioritize keeping your recovery phrase as safe as possible.

# Steps to Setting Up Your Coinbase Application (Hosted Wallet)

1. Download the Coinbase Application.
2. Open the application and click on "Get Started."
3. Use your email address to create an account and press the "Start" button.
4. Verify the email address using the link sent to it.
5. Enter and verify your phone number by way of a code you will have received as a message.
6. Enter your personal details.
7. Fill out your address.
8. Choose the reason why you are utilizing the application.
9. Enter and confirm your income sources and press the "Let's Go" button.
10. Search and link your bank account.
11. Log into your bank account.
12. Select the account to be linked for purchase purposes to your Coinbase App.
13. All done! You are now able to start purchasing cryptocurrencies.

# Chapter 4: The Investor in Context

Not only do you have to know the metaverse and conceptualize it, but you also have to be able to put yourself into context. This way, you will know: who you are as an investor, the types of investment that attract you, your comfortable place in this virtual universe, as well as your approach to it all.

# Choose Your Storage

It is essential to decide on a wallet for storage purposes. The different kinds of storage are cold storage and hot storage. Hot storage refers to storage on online wallets and servers while cold storage refers to offline storage. MetaMask is a software-based hot wallet that does not utilize services for cold storage such as encrypted data servers or hardware wallets. MetaMask is an extremely secure online wallet and has formidable security measures. However, if headlines covering hacked hot wallets make you uneasy, you may worry about the safety of your cryptocurrency wallet.

On the Coinbase Wallet, private keys can be stored offline for Coinbase users. This is a form of storage that is closer to cold storage. Even with this wallet, you do not have to worry about hackers as it also ranks amongst the most secure wallets in the market.

Trust Wallet, on the other hand, has fully cold storage service, which makes it a very attractive mobile app. With this wallet, you will eliminate the need to spend extra on cold storage wallet hardware products. With support for 14 different blockchains, Trust Wallet is a formidable opponent for any cold storage device created. It is essential to note that this cold storage comes as a service, meaning your cryptocurrency is stored offline on secure servers. This is an added security benefit, since it eliminates the risk of you losing your hardware cold storage wallet.

If you have any security issues at heart, then it is advisory to invest in cold storage. The best cold storage wallet in the market right now is Ledger Nano X. With this cold wallet, expect to store all of your private keys securely for just $119. This USB flash drive-like wallet supports over 1,800 cryptocurrencies and it can connect to online devices via Bluetooth or USB.

If you do not have any security concerns, you can utilize cold wallets for long-term investment purposes. This way there is a wallet designated to long-term investment, free from online interference. You can then use your hot wallets for short-term investments.

# Opt for Liquidity

There is no use in investing in an asset on the blockchain that you cannot liquify. This is the very thing that investment is not. To invest means to put your money into an asset that will return financial benefits in the near (or far) future. A good investment opportunity should be able to be the gift that gives independently of the market. This is the case, even though market trends affect investments. It is important to note that the market should not dictate your asset, as this will put you in a vulnerable position as an investor. As such, make investments that can be converted into cash within a short period of time.

The cryptocurrency market fluctuates fast, and when diving into assets backed by these currencies, ensure that the respective cryptocurrency that backs your digital assets is not volatile. This is why it is essential to participate in well-known marketplaces that promote cryptocurrencies that have a proven track record. Simply put, place your digital assets on cryptocurrencies that are in demand.

# Exploit Volatility

When Shiba Inu was introduced into the market, it went volatile really quick. While this is usually seen as a sign to stay away, you can benefit from it. How? It is going to spike up really fast before coming down at the same speed. Therefore, you can buy a new token or coin and wait for its volatility to spike up and then pull your profits out of the position right before it comes back down.

However, this is a task for one who will keep their eye on the ball constantly. This means that you have to monitor your investments closely and set up tools that will prevent loss (where available). You have to keep absorbing information on the coin or token daily from all folds of life. Something as simple as a billionaire putting the name of a cryptocurrency coin or token on their Twitter bio can spike its value up immensely.

# Prioritize Affordability

In our real world, we often know of investment as taking on really steep financial commitments. However, this is not the case with the metaverse. You are able to invest with the little or the plenty that you have. This way, you get to secure your piece of the pie and benefit from it. Therefore, it is essential to rid oneself of the worldly notion that one has to go beyond their means in order to reap gains that are just as huge. In the metaverse, it's a matter of your education and skill. How well do you know your prospective investment opportunity? Because if you know it well enough, you can climb up to your riches from just a modest investment.

Efficiency is the name of the game, and there are no great gains for those who do not prioritize using little input to achieve maximum output. Furthemore, the affordability in this regard is in relation to what you stand to lose. Therefore, avoid putting down an investment that will hurt your livelihood (and those of your loved ones) should you not succeed. The best way to counter steep costs is to use the dollar-cost average method. With the dollar-cost average, you invest a fixed (or certain) amount of money into the metaverse on a monthly basis. This way, you can look into the differing types of investment opportunities at your disposal and decide on a plan to invest in them one by one gradually.

The dollar-cost average method also gives you ample resourcefulness as an investor, since you can get a lot more done this way than through putting down all of your savings at once.

# Withdraw Your Profits

Unless you are utilizing cold storage only, ensure that you withdraw your profits as soon as you become aware of them. The danger with keeping them in there until they gain more is that they might all take a sour turn the very next morning, and you will be greeted with regret. If you have opted for having a cold wallet, the best way to utilize it would be for you to place your profits in it. Holding past your point of profit will just give you more work—you must be careful not to lose your profits. Therefore, you will be tasked with observing external stimuli and absorbing information from every little corner where your investment asset is mentioned.

By regularly withdrawing your profits, you are defining your own entry and exit points. This is a discipline on its own and will add immense value to you personally. If you practice this process religiously, you will not be confused and conflicted by an excess of external stimuli.

# Diversify Your Investment Portfolio

Much like in the real world, you have better chances of financial freedom if you put your fingers in more than just one pie. The metaverse has a lot of interesting avenues to explore, and if you did not end up with just one metaverse investment opportunity, then you are one step into this principle. You can explore all of the investment options that stood out to you throughout this guide.

For instance, you can invest in the Metaverse Index (for a more stable and automatic investment), participate in a play-to-earn game of choice (to earn while having fun), buy stocks from companies that have announced amazing metaverse projects in their pipelines, and maybe look into minting your artwork and listing it on major non-fungible token marketplaces.

# Chapter 5: Equipment Needed to Join the Metaverse

There are a variety of ways through which anyone can enter the metaverse. The way through which one enters the metaverse depends heavily on the kind of metaverse one seeks to join. Since the prevalent feature of almost all of the existing metaverses is to provide users with an extremely interactive environment, special equipment is required. This explains why most gaming metaverses require virtual reality headsets; and most augmented reality experiences require devices with specifications of a higher caliber.

# Virtual Reality Headsets

The first way in which anyone can enter the metaverse is through virtual reality headsets. While virtual headsets have been in the game for a while, the demand for them has increased, mainly because game developers need them in order to simulate fully-immersive adventures for their players. There exists a handful of reliable virtual reality headsets. These are those that pass the quality test by most (if not all) means necessary. However, it should be noted that most gaming virtual reality headsets come prepackaged with demo versions of games chosen or created by the company they are from. This means that a buyer of the headsets will most probably have to make in-app purchases in order to unlock local cryptocurrency games on the headsets. To add to that, a buyer might have to buy games that are not on the headsets (if that particular company supports such games on their device).

It is also important to remember that virtual reality headsets differ in purpose. For instance, there are virtual reality headsets that are focused on being a medium through which a user can experience a virtual reality of choice, while there are those that will come packed with virtual reality content to be bought and unpacked by the buyer. Therefore, it is essential for a prospective buyer to acquaint themself with the purpose that their virtual reality of choice was created to serve. This is to avoid instances of mistaken purchases. As such, please see the listed virtual reality headsets in order to get a better idea of which to go for.

# Oculus Quest 2

With its cinematic sound and high definition display, these virtual reality headsets will make you forget that you are in a simulation. Another star feature of these headsets is that you need only a smartphone and the virtual reality app to get the setup done and dusted. To add to that, it boasts massive memory—giving a buyer an option between 128GB and 256GB. If you are willing to go big, then this company has a wealth of bundles at your disposal. On the other hand, if you do not want to go all out, then you have the option to purchase the headsets only. In both of these instances, a buyer will get value for money.

# HP Reverb G2 VR Headset

With this headset on, each eye of the user has a 2,160 x 2,160 resolution of a screen that comes coupled with an LCD panel. Not only do these specifications make for a highly immersive experience, but they also provide the user with spatial audio as well. These headsets come with four built-in cameras in order to allow users the luxury of monitoring more movement within the virtual experience. HP prioritized comfort when creating this product so that users can enjoy long hours of virtual experiences without discomfort—this is why the headset is flexible and the cushion size is bigger than usual.

# LONGLU VR Headset

Compact and easily foldable, the LONGLU VR Headset is easy to carry around. A user can use these headsets for hours on end without fogging issues and straining their eyes, because they come covered with high-end padding and with lenses that are coated with anti-blue light. If you heavily depend on your glasses for sight, then this product is the right one for you since it is more spacious inside than most of its competitors. This headset has gained its reputation as being beginner-friendly, making it an attractive purchase for first-time virtual reality explorers.

# Pimax Vision 5K Super VR Headset

With a whopping 200-degree field of view, this headset is said to be the closest to human vision. The headset's new design entails a modular head strap and a facial foam pad for ultimate comfort while engaging with the virtual world through a 5,120 x 1,440 resolution display. As if that is not enough, this headset boasts a handful of refresh rate modes of 180Hz, 160Hz, 144Hz, 120Hz, and 90Hz—a feature to earn it a place in the top 5 virtual reality headsets. This headset is one of the top pics for anyone who has their intentions set on experiencing lifelike simulations.

# HTC Vive Pro Fcus Plus

If you do not mind a little workout while gaming or interacting with virtual worlds, then this is the headset for you since it weighs a shocking 2.4 kg (5.42 pounds). Only a select few will be comfortable with carrying this much weight on their heads in the name of adventure. However, these are also the select few who will benefit from its advanced lenses that provide highly immersive video display. The headsets are also made from soft material, which makes the cleaning process less of a hassle. It goes without saying that an easily cleanable piece of equipment is a very usable piece of equipment.

# Valve Index VR HMD

If you fancy anything *but* OLED screens, then this is the headset for you. With 1,440 x 1,600 RGB LCDs, this headset furnishes its user with visuals that are sharper than OLED by more than 50 percent. To add to that, the higher frame rates offer a user with optical comfort and advanced realism. For any prospective buyer, this means longer usage sessions. If it triggers your fancy, you can connect this headset with a computer or USB for an increased performance.

# Feebz VR Headset

If you are not looking to spend big on virtual reality headsets, then this is the headset for you. This headset will provide any beginner with the quality experience of using virtual reality headsets to access and explore virtual worlds. Much like its higher-priced competitors, this headset boasts a spacious inside—allowing for comfortable usage for people who wear glasses for sight. To add to that, it is padded with foam on the inside. This blocks the outside light from piercing into your view while also preventing motion sickness, which deteriorates your experience. The adjustable head straps make for formfitting wear. This headset can also hold a smartphone ranging between 4.7 to 6.5 inches. The star feature of this headset is its 360-degree view, which makes for a highly immersive experience.

# Barbato VR Headset

With a larger than normal lens, this headset offers an increased field of view. This is the feature that has this headset ranked among those with winning displays. With adjustable gears and interpupillary distance, the experience for any user is enjoyable. This headset also provides one of the widest support options for holding smartphones, because it can hold headsets ranging from 3.7 to 7.2 inches. The star feature of this headset is its compatibility with devices such drones, giving its user clarity on the position of the drone at all times.

# Peorpel VR Headset

This headset provides its users with an increased sense of control over their virtual reality experience, mainly due to the fact that the headset comes coupled with a remote controller that you can use to navigate your virtual experience. Its 3AD theater—as well as its 720-degree panoramic view—is what makes this headset stand out as one of the best creations for virtual reality. To add to that, it comes with lenses that are coated with blue light for the protection of your eyes. The make of the model is light and thin, which makes the headsets easier to carry around anywhere. Lastly, it is generously priced, given the high quality specification and features that it boasts.

As can be seen, there exist a variety of headsets. Therefore, one that resonates the most with your value as a user will most probably be the one that stands out to you. In addition to virtual reality headsets, there is augmented reality equipment. Unlike virtual reality headsets, gadgets for augmented reality are aimed mostly at business owners. Augmented reality aims to make corporate, industrial, and other forms of business endeavors a success. This explains the steep pricing of augmented reality gadgets. If you already own a business, or intend on owning one in the near future, then these gadgets will enable a smooth transition into the metaverse for your business.

# Augmented Reality Equipment

# Microsoft HoloLens 2

This mixed reality headset is an asset for precision-focused industries such as health care and manufacturing. What it brings to the table is precision, and this is what makes it an asset for any business. Human error is gravely canceled since human experience will work hand-in-hand with this piece of equipment. If you are wondering how this relates to the metaverse, think of a work day where industry professionals create and interact with blueprints of their product before materializing it. To add to that, think of a day in production where human error is completely eliminated. That is the main purpose of this headset. With the breakthrough that it is making in the industrial metaverse, logic dictates strides as great as Microsoft's XBox to follow this headset's transition into the metaverse.

# Lenovo ThinkReality A3

One of the biggest hurdles for all businesses, especially start-ups, is the expenses associated with renting a place and filling it out with the necessary equipment to make it a suitable workplace. These are the kinds of expenses that deter most business innovations from materializing. However, with equipment such as this, a business owner can bypass all of those expenses and head straight to the business of the day. This is because this gadget is created for the purpose of providing corporations with virtual means of carrying out work. Easily linked to an employee's Windows laptop, this gadget provides users with a large virtual workstation that allows collaboration on organizational goals.

# Magic Leap 1

With the ability to prioritize remote workplace assistance, 3D meetings, and digital work instructions, the Magic Leap 1 is on the list of top equipment for business industries. It is really more of a computer than it is a gadget. Although they can be mistaken for virtual reality headsets, these headsets actually work to intelligently integrate applications into your existing environment. It achieves this seamlessly through its understanding of the world via sophisticated sensors that capture and contour workspace content.

# Smartphone

That's right, your personal smartphone also qualifies as a necessary piece of equipment for interacting with the metaverse. Perfect examples of this truth are your Snapchat and Pokemon GO. On platforms such as these, you need only your smartphone, and then in you go. Your smartphone will not only be useful in the social and gaming metaverses; it will also succeed within the fashion metaverse. This is because the fashion industry depends heavily on augmented reality to give users unique experiences—you can virtually fit your clothing before throwing it into the cart and waiting for the shipment to land.

# Conclusion

As can be seen, the metaverse is ever-expanding in nature. This means it is gradually catering for wider fields of investments, as more digital assets are added to it with every corporation that transitions into the metaverse. Twenty years ago, investing in clothing went as far as the impressions they would help the person buying make and what benefits might arise from those impressions. In today's world, though, an individual can invest in virtual clothing and end up with millions of dollars as return on investment. The world really is changing—and while there exists no monopoly within the metaverse, the safer option for any prospective investor would be to strike while it is still early.

The sense of urgency in making these investments lies solely in the logic that once the masses are on board and the demand increases, supply will require an increase in pricing. Bitcoin, for instance, started off as affordable and accessible. This was because it was still new—and the demand, therefore, was not hectic. However, Bitcoin has grown formidably and is now one of the most expensive investments to make. Investors who joined in on this cryptocurrency while it was still new are reaping immense investment benefits at present. As such, it has set the standard for investing in the metaverse.

Be that as it may, it is easy to make a deadly investment in the haste to secure investment opportunities while they are still affordable. This is the main reason why it is crucial to equip oneself with information on investmenting in the metaverse. As such, absorbing the information and following the practical steps set out within this guide will equip you with enough power to make your first few metaverse investments a success. It goes without saying that what follows the first few investments is personal experience—one of the best ways to gather information. Therefore, this guide will get you in the door—however, it remains your responsibility to merge the fundamental principles shared herein with your personal experience in order to further navigate future investments.

Beware of the dangers of copying other investors' methods and techniques, as the metaverse is mostly user-performance specific—so this might not birth the results you anticipate. Make sure that you find your flow and prioritize your understanding over expert opinion. If you do not understand the dynamic of an investment, it is probably best not to carry it out until you understand. This is why it is advisable to go through this guide more than once. Take this guide as the first investment you will be making in the metaverse, and show up prepared to navigate financial freedom.

At the end of it all, any successful investor has had to study the prospective investment opportunity extensively. Mark Zuckerberg had to invest in knowledge on technology first, navigate it, and then try to advance to what it is today (or what he hopes to build it into since changing Facebook to Meta). So be careful, take your time, and enjoy your exciting investment journey into the metaverse.

# Glossary

*Web 1.0*: This was the first phase of the World Wide Web hosted on pages that were static in nature. The personal web pages in this phase were mostly hosted on web hosting services that were free.

*Web 2.0*: This was the second phase of the World Wide Web that focused on user-generated content. This phase narrowed down its focus from general to user.

*Web 3.0*: This is the third wave of the World Wide Web—it is more of a database than it is a web. Within this web data is shared and not owned. To add to that, differing views on the same data are also shown by the services within this version of the web.

*Database*: This is organized and structured information that users can access, update, modify, manage, and control easily. This information is usually stored electronically.

*Metaverse*: This term is usually used to refer to a virtual universe in which other virtual worlds exist or are being created.

*Virtual reality*: This is a reality created wholly by a computer and has 3D simulations of images and environments that can be interacted with. The interactions usually seem real for users who interact through specialized equipment.

*Augmented reality*: This is a reality created partially by a computer and it has 3D simulations of images and environments that can be interacted with. The reality is partial because it creates simulations of realities in the real world.

*Avatar*: This is a virtual representation of the user within a certain virtual world. It is the virtual body through which a user experiences the virtual experiences.

*Multiplayer*: This is a gaming system that allows more than one player to participate in its activities simultaneously.

*Blockchain*: This is a technology that uses ledger-like systems of recording transactions made using cryptocurrency. This system is mained by a network of computers associated by peer-to-peer review.

# References


The Ascent Staff. (2022, February 17). *Best NFT marketplaces*. The Motley Fool. https://www.fool.com/the-ascent/cryptocurrency/nft-marketplaces[1]

Bardi, J. (2020, September 21). *What is virtual reality? [Definition and examples]*. Marxent. https://www.marxentlabs.com/wp-content/uploads/2018/10/marxLogo397x58.png. https://www.marxentlabs.com/what-is-virtual-reality[2]

Binance Blog. (2019, January 23). *Trust Wallet 2.0: One app for all your crypto*. Binance.com. https://www.binance.com/en/blog/all/trust-wallet-20-one-app-for-all-your-crypto-2950634536823 11168

Coin Introduction. (n.d.). *Social network for programmers and developers*. Morioh.com. https://morioh.com/p/4bbb9ad26c1b

Coinbase. (n.d.). *How to set up a crypto wallet*. Coinbase.com. https://www.coinbase.com/learn/tips-and-tutorials/how-to-set-up-a-crypto-wallet

Cox, D. (2022, January 13). *Coinbase wallet review 2022*. Cryptonewsz.com. https://www.cryptonewsz.com/crypto-wallet/coinbase-wallet-review[3]


---

1. https://www.fool.com/the-ascent/cryptocurrency/nft-marketplaces/

2. https://www.marxentlabs.com/what-is-virtual-reality/

3. https://www.cryptonewsz.com/crypto-wallet/coinbase-wallet-review/

Decentralizedcreator. (2021, December 5). *How to create a metamask wallet: A step by step guide.* DecentralizedCreator.com. https://decentralizedcreator.com/create-metamask-wallet[4]

Freeman Law. (2020). *Mining explained: A detailed guide on how cryptocurrency mining works.* FreemanLaw.com. https://freemanlaw.com/mining-explained-a-detailed-guide-on-how-cryptocurrency-mining-works[5]

Gailey, A. (2022, February 14). *3 Experts explain why NFTs are so popular, and what they mean for crypto investors.* Time. https://time.com/nextadvisor/investing/cryptocurrency/are-nfts-good-investment[6]

Geeks for Geeks. (2022, January 27). *Web 1.0, web 2.0 and web 3.0 with their difference.* GeeksforGeeks.org. https://www.geeksforgeeks.org/web-1-0-web-2-0-and-web-3-0-with-their-difference/

Gosavi, A. (2022, January 19). *9 Virtual reality headsets to enjoy the exciting world of metaverse.* Interesting Engineering. https://interestingengineering.com/9-virtual-reality-headsets-to-enjoy-the-exciting-world-of-metaverse

Haselton, T. (2021, April 14). *Here's what Coinbase is and how to use it to buy and sell cryptocurrencies.* CNBC. https://www.cnbc.com/2021/04/14/what-is-coinbase-how-to-use-it.html

---

4. https://decentralizedcreator.com/create-metamask-wallet/

5. https://freemanlaw.com/mining-explained-a-detailed-guide-on-how-cryptocurrency-mining-works/

6. https://time.com/nextadvisor/investing/cryptocurrency/are-nfts-good-investment/

Hore-Thorburn, I. (2021). *NFT innovators RTFKT just secured $8 million in funding.* Highsnobiety. https://www.highsnobiety.com/p/rtfkt-funding-digital-supreme[7]

Kastrenakes, J. (2021, March 11). *Beeple sold an NFT for $69 million.* The Verge. https://www.theverge.com/2021/3/11/22325054/beeple-christies-nft-sale-cost-everydays-69-million

MetaMask. (n.d.). *FAQs | MetaMask.* Metamask.io. https://metamask.io/faqs[8]

Oracle. (2020). *What is a database?.* Oracle.com. https://www.oracle.com/za/database/what-is-database/

Oxford Languages. (2021). *Oxford Languages and Google - English.* Oxford University Press. https://languages.oup.com/google-dictionary-en[9]

Patterson, D. (2021, December 8). *Gateway to the metaverse: Top AR glasses and VR headsets you can buy right now.* CBS News. https://www.cbsnews.com/news/metaverse-ar-glasses-vr-headset-apps[10]

Quast, J. (2022, February 2). *Investing in metaverse stocks.* The Motley Fool. https://www.fool.com/investing/stock-market/market-sectors/information-technology/metaverse-stocks[11]

---

7. https://www.highsnobiety.com/p/rtfkt-funding-digital-supreme/

8. https://metamask.io/faqs/

9. https://languages.oup.com/google-dictionary-en/

10. https://www.cbsnews.com/news/metaverse-ar-glasses-vr-headset-apps/

11. https://www.fool.com/investing/stock-market/market-sectors/information-technology/metaverse-stocks/

Rosenberg, E. (2022, February 15). *Crypto.com review.* Investopedia. https://www.investopedia.com/crypto-com-review-5209370

TechTarget Contributor. (n.d.). *Augmented reality gaming (AR gaming).* WhatIs.com. https://whatis.techtarget.com/definition/augmented-reality-gaming-AR-gaming

Watson, T. (2021, November 18). *3D Avatars in the metaverse: Everything you need to know.* https://skywell.software/blog/3d-avatars-in-the-metaverse-everything-you-need-to-know

WTOP News. (2021, November 9). *The 8 best cryptocurrency wallets.* WTOP.com. https://wtop.com/news/2021/11/the-8-best-cryptocurrency-wallets/

www.ingramcontent.com/pod-product-compliance
Lightning Source LLC
Chambersburg PA
CBHW051248160726
47994CB00003B/1068